The Smart & Easy Guide To Loans: The Complete Guide Book To Your Credit Score, Home Financing, Mortgages, Car Loans, Student Loans, Credit Repair, Credit Cards & Payday Loans

Darryl Johnson

Legal Stuff

Copyright Information

Copyright © 2013 Checkmate Marketing Group LLC. All rights reserved worldwide.

No part of this publication may be replicated, redistributed, or given away in any form without the prior written consent of the publisher.

Checkmate Marketing Group LLC

Earnings Disclaimer

EVERY EFFORT HAS BEEN MADE TO ACCURATELY REPRESENT THIS PRODUCT AND IT'S POTENTIAL. IN TERMS OF EARNINGS, THERE IS NO GUARANTEE THAT YOU WILL EARN ANY MONEY USING THE TECHNIQUES AND IDEAS IN THIS MATERIAL. INFORMATION PRESENTED ON THIS BOOK IS NOT TO BE INTERPRETED AS A PROMISE OR GUARANTEE OF EARNINGS. EARNING POTENTIAL IS ENTIRELY DEPENDENT ON THE PERSON USING OUR PRODUCT, IDEAS AND TECHNIQUES.

ANY CLAIMS MADE OF ACTUAL EARNINGS OR EXAMPLES OF ACTUAL RESULTS CAN BE VERIFIED UPON REQUEST. YOUR LEVEL OF SUCCESS IN ATTAINING THE RESULTS CLAIMED IN OUR MATERIALS DEPENDS ON THE TIME YOU DEVOTE TO THE PROGRAM, IDEAS AND TECHNIQUES MENTIONED, YOUR FINANCES, KNOWLEDGE AND VARIOUS SKILLS. SINCE THESE FACTORS DIFFER ACCORDING TO INDIVIDUALS, WE CANNOT GUARANTEE YOUR SUCCESS OR INCOME LEVEL.

ANY AND ALL FORWARD LOOKING STATEMENTS HERE OR ON ANY OF OUR SALES MATERIAL ARE INTENDED TO EXPRESS OUR OPINION OF EARNINGS POTENTIAL. MANY FACTORS WILL BE IMPORTANT IN DETERMINING YOUR ACTUAL RESULTS AND NO GUARANTEES ARE MADE THAT YOU WILL ACHIEVE RESULTS SIMILAR TO OURS OR ANYONE ELSES. NO GUARANTEES ARE MADE THAT YOU WILL ACHIEVE ANY RESULTS FROM OUR IDEAS AND TECHNIQUES IN OUR MATERIAL.

Limitation of Liability

THE MATERIALS IN THIS BOOK ARE PROVIDED "AS IS" WITHOUT ANY EXPRESS OR IMPLIED WARRANTY OF ANY KIND INCLUDING WARRANTIES OF MERCHANTABILITY, NONINFRINGEMENT OF INTELLECTUAL PROPERTY, OR FITNESS FOR ANY PARTICULAR PURPOSE. IN NO EVENT SHALL OR ITS AGENTS OR OFFICERS BE LIABLE FOR ANY DAMAGES WHATSOEVER (INCLUDING, WITHOUT LIMITATION, DAMAGES FOR LOSS OF PROFITS, BUSINESS INTERRUPTION, LOSS OF INFORMATION, INJURY OR DEATH) ARISING OUT OF THE USE OF OR INABILITY TO USE THE MATERIALS, EVEN IF HAS BEEN ADVISED OF THE POSSIBILITY OF SUCH LOSS OR DAMAGES.

Table of Contents

Introduction 6
Part 1: Your Credit Report 7
Part 2: Mortgages 16
Part 3: Car Loans 25
Part 4: Student Loans 28
Part 5: Credit Cards 37
Part 6: Payday Lenders, Loaning to Friends, and Other Special Situations 44
Conclusion 51
We Want Your Feedback on This Book! 52

Introduction

Sometimes, you just need money. Going to college, buying a house, financing a car – no matter what major life choice you're preparing to make, you'll probably need to take out a loan.

But signing for a loan can be full of pitfalls and dangers. Beyond the fine print, there are fees, interest rates, deadlines, and a million other details that seem designed to confuse. Getting help with loans can be worse. Where can a non-banker turn for loan advice these days?

Luckily, you've got in your hands a quick guide to getting, managing, and living with your loan. By using the advice in this book, you'll learn to take advantage of the best loans and avoid becoming overwhelmed with bad ones. The peace of mind you'll enjoy when you're informed will let you make difficult loan decisions confidently, avoiding beginners' mistakes and using your knowledge to achieve your dreams.

Part 1: Your Credit Report

It may surprise you to learn just how much of your credit history is available to lenders. To put it succinctly, a lender can see everything about your credit – including some things that might surprise you!

Chapter 1. Need money? Know your options!

Before you seek a loan, you should do some research – on you! Your credit rating, which covers a shocking amount of your past financial activity, can tattletale on your finances.

If you find yourself rejected for a loan after laboring for hours over your loan paperwork, then the reason probably has something to do with your credit rating. A poor or odd-looking credit report can hurt your chances for getting a loan, or even disqualify you completely. A bank or lending institution can pull up your credit information any time they want to – and they always will, too.

This seems a little unfair! After all, that credit report isn't exactly coming to your mailbox with your monthly bank statement. Maybe you weren't even aware of your credit before you were turned down for a loan. What is this thing, anyway? How did you get one?

A credit report is a summary of your credit rating that is available to financial institutions on demand. Everyone has a credit rating. Your rating reflects all of your personal financial history, from how regularly you pay your bills to how many credit cards you have. To a banker or other money expert, your financial report is key. A lender will lend or not lend to you based mostly on that report.

If you want a loan, you'd better know what's in your report. Know how it works for you, how it works against you, and, most importantly, know what's on it!

Four Things that are Definitely on Your Credit Report

As a wise man once said, knowledge is power. Knowing about your credit report ahead of time can save you all kinds of disappointment at the bank.

1. Your Personal Information

First and foremost, your credit report includes everything about you. This is called your *personal information.*

Your personal information is probably fairly familiar to you. It includes your full name, your social security number, and everywhere you've ever lived and worked. You're probably fairly used to seeing all of this information around and may even consider it common knowledge. But it's very important to make sure that the information that you give to the bank matches what's on your credit report. All of the personal information on your credit report was gathered from your past creditors, and they keep track!

2. Your Public Records

Aside form the tabs that creditors have been keeping on you, there's plenty of information on your financial history in the *public record*. The public record keeps track of any bankruptcies or foreclosures that you've ever experienced, as well as any accounts that you might have in collection.

Your public record shows up on your credit report in a big way. Lending institutions are generally very interested in your public record information, so be aware!

3. Your Credit History

Anyone reading your credit report will be able to see how many and what kinds of accounts you have. Accounts include all of your credit cards, student loans, car payments – in fact, it includes all of the loans you've ever had!

It should go without saying that your credit report shows your payment history, too. If you've ever missed a payment on any of your accounts, then this will show up on your credit report. If you've missed too many payments on past loans, then future lenders might deny your loan request.

4. Your Credit Inquiries

Believe it or not, your credit report also tells lenders how often you've asked for a loan in the past. Any time you file an inquiry for a new line of credit, whether a credit card or a mortgage, that request shows up on your credit report.

If you make too many requests in too short a period of time, lenders will get suspicious. They might think that you're shopping around for a better deal. You'll look like a bad risk to them. Filing a lot of inquiries all at once is a surefire way to get denied for loans in the future.

Chapter 2. Your Credit Score

After your lender looks over your credit report, the next thing they'll be interested in is your *credit score*. This number, which is mathematically derived from your credit report, falls between 300 and 850. The higher your credit score, the better your chance of getting a loan.

Not only can your credit report have a huge impact on your ability to secure a loan, but your credit report can affect the terms under which you receive a loan offer. If your credit rating is poor, then you're likelier to see a high interest rate on your loan than you would if your rating were good. Other loan terms can go against you too. At worst, every lender you approach will reject your application when they see your poor credit report.

This is why it's critically important to secure a copy of your credit report before you apply for a loan. You want to have time to correct any of your past debt management issues before a lender sees it. Don't wait until after you've added to your problems by making a bunch of no-go loan inquiries.

Luckily, there are several agencies that can pull your credit report for you on demand. They are easy to locate on the Internet, and in fact, some of them may be able to produce a basic credit report for you online.

There are also a few different types of credit reports available. The basic report includes the information that we talked about in Chapter 1. More detailed reports may include your current credit score or a side-by-side comparison of your standing with all three of the major credit reporting agencies.

You may find yourself surprised with the results, particularly if you decide to run your credit report through more than one company. Even if your credit is OK, you may end up with three different reports. In this case, the problem isn't with you, but with your credit report. Maybe your personal information is out of date or contains incorrect information. Though an old address may not seem like a big deal to you, your bank may have questions about any odd little mistakes. Avoiding questions is a great reason to close any gaps between what's on the report and what's on your application. If your lender is particularly curious about your history, their inquiries could prolong the loaning process and leave you high and dry – and without a loan – for weeks.

Be sure to take a close look at your credit report and correct any mistakes as soon as you see them. Remember, credit reporting agencies work independently of one another. They never share information, even if it's important to your loan process. If you want to be absolutely sure that your information is accurate, you'll need to contact each credit agency individually. It's a pain, but it's worth it in the long run!

Your report also includes some commentary from your past lenders. That's important too: any comments on your report will affect your buying and borrowing power for seven to ten years. Positive comments can help you out a lot, functioning just like a good recommendation to future lender. But if your credit report includes a negative comment, then watch out! Even if the comment isn't accurate, it can hurt your chances of getting a loan. Do your best to avoid accumulating negative comments.

Your credit report is a great reminder to make all of your financial decisions very cautiously. Be especially careful with your debt, credit cards, and student loans. Even minor financial accidents can show up on your credit report forever.

Don't let a naive mistake prevent you from fulfilling your dreams! Know your credit report inside and out before you even approach a lender.

Chapter 3. High Score, Low Interest: the art of credit scoring

Credit scoring is a system that can help improve your credit score. With a better score, you'll see lower interest rates, more loan offers, and even better rates on insurance.

We mentioned your credit score briefly in Chapter 2. It's a critical and somewhat cryptic number that shows up a lot in commercials. But what exactly is a credit score? Why can't your score be greater than 850 or less than 300? And where does your credit score come from?

Though these questions may sound daunting, the answers are fairly straightforward. Credit bureaus calculate your credit score based on your financial history. Your credit score determines how much money a lender will loan you, how high your monthly payments will be, your interest, and a number of other factors. After your credit report, it's the single most important factor in securing a good loan.

Several factors contribute to your credit score. Your credit and debt history is extremely important, as well as how many accounts you have open and how long you've maintained them. Each factor is worth a certain number of points. Some factors, such as your outstanding debt, are worth more points than others.

Once they've determined how many points you have in each category, the credit bureau adds everything up. That lump sum is your credit score. The more points you have, the higher your credit score, and the higher your credit score, the more likely you are to get a good offer on a loan.

There are several ways to keep your credit score high. The best is to always pay your bills on time. One of the most important factors in your credit score is how regularly you pay off your debts.

Also, be conscious of how you use credit, including credit cards. Taking advantage of credit responsibly can make your credit score look fantastic. Demonstrating that you can pay off small, regular debts with no problem indicates that you're a safe bet for a more serious loan. Using and paying off credit regularly will give your credit score a big boost.

You're also more likely to get a loan if you have a long credit history. This is especially true if you've managed lots of different kinds of credit. This will show lenders that you can handle the pressure of a loan, even if you have other things going on in your life.

It's all well and good to learn about your credit score now, but if your score has already taken some damage, you'll need to take steps to improve it as soon as possible. Luckily, you have a few options.

First, obtain your credit report. This isn't too hard – in fact, you can get a free credit report over the Internet. Equifax, Experian, and Trans-Union are credit agencies that offer a free yearly credit report. Several other agencies can offer you multiple reports per year, though they are more likely to charge for this service.

Getting your credit report won't hurt your chances of getting a loan, but asking for it too much will negatively affect your credit score. That means that the more often you ask for your credit report, the lower your credit score will become. Remember, the more inquiries you make into your credit, the worse you'll look to lenders.

Next, check all of the information on your credit report carefully. If you find any inaccuracies, dispute them as soon as you can. You must file a dispute within 30 days of receiving your credit report or it won't be investigated.

The good news is that if you do report an error, your credit score will get a bump automatically. This is because updating your information prevents errors ranging from inaccurate reporting to identity theft. Correcting your personal info isn't just good for you – it's a public service!

You also have the right to dispute negative comments on your credit report. If you can prove your case, this process can completely remove a bad comment. If you dispute a comment but can't get it erased, don't despair. In a year or two, it will probably come off your record anyway. Check up on your credit report annually, just to make sure.

Last but not least, look over your credit report for accounts or collections that are past due. Paying off your outstanding debts will have a dramatic positive impact on your credit score. Be aware that some agencies won't fix your report until after you've paid them, so the more of your debt that you can pay off, the better. Aim to pay right before a lender reports to the credit agency. By the time the report comes through, you'll already have decreased your debt.

Chapter 4. Pay it off!

Getting right by your credit report is often just a matter of paying your debts. In the golden age of the credit card, this is much easier said than done! Whatever your situation, do not despair. You CAN cut down your debt and improve your credit score. The fact that you're even trying will make you look like a better loan candidate immediately, even if it can't guarantee you instant success in actually securing one.

We'll talk more about credit cards and credit card deb in Part 5. But with any loan, having a plan is key. Figure out how much you owe, how long it will take you to repay, and what you need to do to get that debt off your record.

Part 2: Mortgages

Mortgages are major life decisions that almost everyone who buys a house must make. Though they seem complicated at first, you'll catch on fast once you learn the parlance.

Chapter 5. Speak the Same Language: learn the lingo of mortgages

Loans come in different shapes, sizes, and categories, all with unique special features. They often feature unique special words, too. In this chapter, we'll discuss some basic loan lingo as applicable to home loans.

Home loans are also called *mortgages.* They're extremely common and available for almost all income brackets. As such, there are a few different kinds.

Government loans: The United States has a large presence on the residential mortgage market. About 20 percent of home loans are either guaranteed or insured by an agency of the U.S. federal government. These federally-guaranteed loans are called *government loans*.

Conventional loans: The other 80 percent of residential mortgages are *conventional loans*. They aren't provided by the U.S. Government, but by private, and often for-profit, lenders.

Though the money for conventional loans comes from banks and other private financial institutions, they still usually have a close relationship with the government. This is because mortgages are a huge risk even for very large institutions. The U.S. Government insures many conventional mortgages. That way, even if the loan isn't paid, the lender still gets their money back. It's a good incentive to offer a loan to someone who might otherwise look like a poor candidate.

Federal Housing Administration (FHA): Founded in 1934, which was during the depths of the Great Depression, the FHA's purpose was originally to encourage the growth of the then-ailing U.S. housing industry. Today, this body encourages people of low or moderate income to get mortgages. It does this by providing insurance to lenders who make FHA loans.

The FHA itself is not a money lender. To get an FHA loan, borrowers must look for an FHA-approved lender. This is usually a bank or other financial institution.

Department of Veterans Affairs (VA): The Department of Veterans' Affairs enables military personnel on active duty and military veterans to buy homes. Like the FHA, the VA does not itself loan money, but guarantees mortgages and loans granted by other lending institutions. VA loans offer competitive interest rates, little or no down payments, and very little declaration of income.

Farmers Home Administration (FHA): Yes, that's the same acronym as the one for the Federal Housing Administration! We weren't kidding when we said you'd want to know the lingo. Imagine the mix-ups this has caused!

Contrary to its name, you don't have to be a farmer to obtain an FHA loan. However, the home you're mortgaging needs to be located in a rural area. These loans come with minimal down payment and are easier to obtain than others. To make matters more confusing, these FHA loans are also overseen by the other FHA – that is, the Federal Housing Administration.

Farmers Home Administration loans come with many attractive features, including minimal cash down payments, long loan terms, lower interest rates, and some extra perks that kick in if you repay your loan before its deadline.

The downside is that these loans have comparatively low maximum mortgage amounts. They also take a very long time to process. For their target clientele, though, they're often worth the wait.

These are three fairly basic types of loans that you'll find everywhere. However, you'll run into a number of different types of loan wherever you go, including these.

Fixed rate loans: Notoriously easy to get, fixed rate loans include a 20- or 30-year repayment plan. Though it's a long haul, it also means that your payments will be a little easier on your pocketbook. If you plan to live in your home for several years, this loan is for you. It's also the top pick for people looking to live on a budget.

Adjustable rate mortgages (ARMs): Though this loan scheme has a low adjustable rate, it is not unusual for lenders to insist on a maximum repayment period of just 10 years. The rule of thumb is that you'll start paying this loan off sooner.

Combination (hybrid) loans: These loans feature a combination of features typical of both fixed rate and ARMs. They have a built-in delayed adjustment period, though the initial loan period is fixed. Combination loans carry very little risk, and their interest rates are usually much smaller than what you'd expect to see on a fixed rate loan. Though they begin as fixed rate loans, they basically become ARMs, adjustable rate and all, after a few years.

Combination loans are best for people who are on the move. This is because interest rates on these loans are very low for the first few years – enough time to unload a starter house on a future long-term resident without paying too much on it yourself.

Balloon mortgages: Mortgage installments for balloon mortgages are based on a fixed term of up to 30 or 15 years amortization. That means that you can take your time paying the loan for a while. But at the end of that "balloon" period, it's time to pay back the rest – no matter how much you've got left.

Pledge asset mortgages: Pledged asset mortgages are loans meant for people with significant income and investments. In place of a cash down payment on this mortgage, the person looking for the loan can pledge their investments as collateral.

Chapter 6. The ABCs of Finance

As we've already seen, the world of finance readily dissolves into a bewildering alphabet soup. The ABCs of finance are usually technical and not very interesting, but in a few minutes, you'll be slinging acronyms like a pro.

All of the acronyms we talk about here have to do with your loans. You'll definitely want to study them before you go in for your loan, because your lender already knows them by heart!

APR stands for *Annual Percentage Rate.* This is the yearly cost of a loan, boiled down to a single fee that is a percentage of your payment. Your APR includes both interest and insurance. It is most likely to be included in mortgages, credit cards and car financing. Knowing a loan's APR should very important to your loan choice.

As far as credit cards are concerned, there are a couple of different types of APRs that you're likely to run into. The first covers purchases that you make using your card. This type is the lowest APR you're likely to ever see. If you have to take a loan or cash advance out of your credit line, or if you go over your credit limit, your APR will automatically increase. Making a balance transfer from one credit card to another will increase your APR.

There are many other forms of APR that apply to everyday loans, and it's important to be aware of all of them. Tiered APRs will apply different rates to certain levels of your outstanding balance. Penalty APRs can make past-due loans much larger than they seem, and can kick in as soon as the first time you miss a credit card payment.

If you already have an APR, you can always try to get it lowered. There are several ways to do this. If you're looking for a mortgage, you can negotiate closing costs and keep your mortgage for longer. This will automatically drop the APR to fit with the extended time period and your annual rate.

FICO stands for the Fair Isaac Credit Organization. The Fair Isaac Corporation is a company that provides several different financial services, including mortgages, insurance, and healthcare. FICO is one of their branches. You can get your credit score and good credit advice through this company. If you are applying for a new loan or credit card, your lenders will most often go to FICO to get your credit score.

HELOC stands for home equity line of credit. HELOC is mainly used for taking out a mortgage or a home loan and features a larger amount of credit with a lower interest rate. This type of credit line is also usually based around a variable interest rate.

A variable interest rate is a rate that changes in reaction to an interest rate that's considered standard in your economy, such as the U.S. Treasury Bond Yield. Because your loan's variable interest rate can go up or down depending on how the economy fares, it's a good idea to look into the index and margin that each lender uses before going for your loan. Also, look into the interest rate's cap, or maximum size. Obviously, you want the lowest cap possible for your loan.

The amount of credit you will receive in a HELOC is usually based on a percentage of the appraised value of your home. Your ability to repay the loan will also be considered. Factors like debt, income, and credit history will all contribute to the amount of credit that you receive. Once you're approved, you'll be able to draw from your HELOC as you would from a bank account, though there may be limits on how much you can take out at once. Be aware: if you decide to sell your home, you will probably have to pay back the HELOC in full.

Knowledge is power. No matter what kind of loan or credit line you're trying to get, having some background on how loans work is the crucial factor in your success.

Chapter 7. Allow for Amortization

Amortization is a term that you don't hear all that often compared to, say "credit score" and "APR." But amortization is something that everyone does. In fact, you may be doing it right now.

Amortization is when you periodically pay off a loan. The loan can be anything from a car, goods, furniture, or anything else you've bought on credit. Paying a mortgage on your own home is a form of amortization. Interestingly enough, the words "mortgage" and "amortization" both include the root word 'mort,' which means "kill." That fits perfectly because it's exactly what you're doing: you are paying off your loan until it has been eliminated – killed to death and gone for good.

The process of amortization is simple once you know the basics. Over a set number of periodical payments, you will eliminate your loan. A typical payment factors in the size of your loan, (AKA your principle,) the amount of payments you'll make, and the loan's interest rate.

For example, let's say you bought a home worth $150,000. Obviously you're getting a loan for that, and after some shopping around and negotiating, you put down a $20,000 deposit on a 30 year loan with an interest rate of 7%. You're left with a principle of $130,000.

Sounds great! But how much will you pay each month?

Loan math isn't exactly straightforward. The following formula will produce your monthly payment:

[interest rate + interest rate / ((1 + interest rate) ^ months - 1)] x principal loan amount = Your Monthly Payment

Easy, right? The upshot is that for your 30 year loan, you'll initially pay a total of about $864.89 per month. If you're especially math-savvy, you'll notice another interesting fact: your interest will total $181,361.57 over that thirty year amortization! In fact, your interest will initially cost you $758.33 of that monthly $864.89. Every payment you make will go toward your interest first, too. This is how your loan can go "under water," which happens when your monthly payments are too low to have an impact on your principle.

That may sound pretty bleak, but there's good news too! As you pay off your principle, your interest per payment will also decrease. For example, let's say you've just made your 200th successful payment. Your principle is down to $90,143.37 and your calculated interest reflects that decrease. Though your payment is the same – still $864.89 – your interest is down to a paltry $525.84. The rest goes toward your principle – you're paying it off faster than ever!

Soon your principle payments will be bigger than your interest. At Payment 300, you'll take out a healthy $606.56 of your principle and a piddling $258.33 in interest. At Payment 359, you'll fork over just $10 to your loan's interest as you prepare to slay that loan for good.

Remember, your payment is always the same. You'll just make more headway against your principle as you go along.

Loans are a deceptively large commitment and it can be difficult to decide just how much you can afford to pay. Luckily, a number of amortization calculators are available for free on the internet. Use them to help you work out your monthly cost before you take out a loan. Some lenders also employ in-house accountants who will help you to break down your payment requirements.

Part 3: Car Loans

Car loans are a headache, not just because they are fairly tricky as loans go, but because cars aren't great investments. If yours breaks before your loan is finished, then you may find yourself face-to-face with an all-too-common problem...

Chapter 8. Upside Down on a Car Loan: avoid owing more than your car is worth

You did everything right when you took out your car loan, but now that car is breaking down...and you still have more than two years of car payments left. Congratulations: you are now "upside down." That means that you owe more on a car loan than your car is actually worth.

The true cost of your car is much higher than the sticker price, and learning about it ahead of time is one of the best things you can do for your financial health. Otherwise, you'll find yourself in a downward spiral of loan payments, repair costs, gas and maintenance that eat up your cash while you pay for living expenses on credit. Your debt snowballs, your credit tanks, and it's all the fault of that lemon of a car that you no longer want.

The key is to keep your car loan under control. To put it simply, do the math before you do anything else. Calculate the maximum loan that you could sustain based on your income and try to look for a car that will outlast that loan. Once upon a time, 36 months was considered the standard loan period, but these days dealers have extended car installment loans to 60 or even 72 months.

Though it may seem to be a better idea to opt for a longer car loan period, you're also much more likely to purchase a car you can't afford. Remember, the longer your loan's amortization time is, the more interest you'll pay. Buying a new vehicle isn't a great idea either; your old loan just gets rolled into your new one and your interest rates end up even higher than before.

On top of all this, your car's value will depreciate, or decrease as you use it, much faster than you can pay it off. Cars, especially new cars, are notorious for losing value fast. You've probably heard jokes about how they drop in resale value as soon as they're driven off the lot. That's no joke! If you take out a 60 month car loan, you'll soon owe more on your loan than your car is technically worth. With additional repair costs and gas, never mind tire changes and insurance, your car loan turns your originally useful vehicle into a full-on financial black hole.

That's why it's critical to choose a short-term loan period. Be pragmatic about what you can really afford. Come to the dealership armed with cold, hard figures and don't compromise on your finances. Experts advise that you pay no more than 15% of your income on your car loan. For example, if your monthly take-home pay is $3,000, then your monthly car payment should not exceed $450.

Look beyond the sticker price when you shop for a car. What does insurance cost for different makes and models? You might be surprised at the difference between premiums for a flashy sports car verses a modest sedan. What type of repair costs can you expect? Which cars have the best fuel economy? All of those figures should go into your calculations before you head to the car lot!

Finally, consider your needs. Do you really have to buy a new car? It's a tremendous financial headache and, unlike a house, there's very little you can do to prevent its value from depreciating. In fact, the value of a new car often plummets by 30 to 40 percent in the first two years of ownership!

A used car may be a better choice, though you'll need to do more research. Being cheaper, these cars may include a shorter loan period, or even be inexpensive enough to pay for up front. Imagine the peace of mind you'll experience when you have no car loan to worry about!

If you must absolutely buy a new car, hold on to it for a few years. This may help you to absorb extra costs in the long run. But approach any car loan with extreme caution. Do as much research ahead of time as you possibly can! Remember, no matter what the car salesman tells you, your finances aren't that flexible. This loan will affect you for a long time and it's worth a LOT of thought.

Part 4: Student Loans

Let's face it: if you're going to school, you're probably getting a loan. This may be your first major credit transaction, but don't worry! You'll be glad you did it.

Chapter 9. Study your Options

Going to school has never been more expensive or more necessary. Taking out student loans has become standard operating procedure for thousands of young adults nationwide. Unfortunately, most young people have little or no experience with finance, much less with personal debt and credit. They know they need money – that much is obvious – but the pitfalls of student loans are often lost upon them.

If you're a student looking at taking out a loan, then good on you! You're doing the right thing by educating yourself about this complicated process. Make sure and take advantage of your financial aid counselor and your parents. You may even want to hire a professional to debrief you. Some private financial advisors charge by the hour, and even $50 for a 30-minute session is worth more than what an innocent mistake could cost you in the future.

Attending college is expensive in every sense. Tuition, various fees, your dorm room, that delicious dining hall food, books – all of this and more can send your college expenses through the stratosphere. According to the College Board, the total cost of college for this past academic year – just one year, remember – averaged $11,000 for a two year college and $14,000 for a four year college. Remember, depending on where you attend school, you need two or *four* of those just to get an Associate's or Bachelor's degree! Private colleges, which include the Ivy League schools, can cost $30,000 per year or more.

To make matters worse, college tuition responds to changes in the inflation rate very quickly. As a result, the cost of school grows by between five and eight percent every year. Some estimates find that the cost of college doubles about every nine years.

Scholarships and loans are usually important keys to higher education. Getting a loan is very easy, but it's extremely important to consider the terms, have a plan, and choose your loan wisely.

Federal aid is one of the most common ways to get a student loan. Instead of borrowing from a private institution, you'll borrow tuition money from the U.S. Government itself. as opposed to private lenders. When you file for a federal student loan, your financial needs will be determined and the amount of aid you receive will be based on that. There is over $67 billion dollars available in federal student loans nationally.

In order to qualify for a federal student loan, you must have a high school diploma, take a certain number of credit hours per semester, maintain a high grade point average, and be an U.S citizen.

The **Stafford Loan** is one of the most popular federal student loans available. The student starts paying this loan back six months after graduation. Interest rates on Stafford loans are usually relatively low.

Stafford loans come subsidized and unsubsidized. **Subsidized loans** are offered to students based on their financial need. As long as the student is enrolled at least half time in the university and has financial need, they qualify for a subsidized loan. Unlike other forms of student loans, the U.S. Government pays the accruing interest on this loan while the student is taking classes.

Unsubsidized loans are not dependent on financial need. They will begin building up interest while the student is still taking classes, and after graduation, whoever took out the loan is responsible for everything. Unsubsidized loans also require that the parents pay off a certain amount of the loan within a given amount of time.

Campus-based aid programs are also popular where federal aid doesn't cover the entire cost of school. These usually come in the form of either loans or grants bestowed by a school. However, the money for campus-based aid programs also comes from the federal government. Instead of giving aid money to students, the government gives it to the school and allows them to divide it up as they see fit. If you receive campus-based aid, you will be eligible for work study, which gives you a job on campus, a grant, or a Federal Perkins Loan. Like many other forms of federally-sourced student aid, campus-based assistance is usually dependent on your income.

You can apply for all federal loans online through the FAFSA website. Applications are due at the beginning of March, but it's a good idea to get them in early. As soon as your eligibility is determined, you will receive a letter in the mail that tells you what loans you qualify for and how much money you can expect to receive. Then, you have the option of accepting or declining each of your options. While it might be tempting to accept as much as you want, remember: you're paying all of this back someday, with interest. Choose your loans wisely.

Private student loans are also available. Most of the time, they feature much higher interest rates and fairly unfavorable terms, but if your federal loans just don't cover your costs, they are an option.

If you must take out private loans, shop around. This will be a massive headache. You'll fill out forms, read fine print, grill lenders, and drive yourself crazy trying to negotiate favorable conditions. Don't give up! Someday soon, you'll be glad you went to all this trouble.

Loans are supposed to get you through college easier, but like any credit transaction, you will need to pay them off. Be prepared and plan!

Chapter 10. Kids in College Can Be a PLUS: Parents, know your education funding Options

This part is for parents who are sending their kids to school. Many parents help their children for a while, and that help can help alleviate your student's need to take out student loans. On the other hand, you may end up taking out a loan yourself!

Finding a quality school should be your first priority, but affordability shouldn't be far behind. Consider your student's living expenses, too. Your student is unlikely to have a great job during school, even if they've worked throughout high school. Expect to support your child for a few more years.

If you took the long view 18 years ago, then you may have already started a savings account for your kids' education. If you're reading ahead, so to speak, then now's a great time to open a **Coverdell Education Savings Account**, also known as an **Education IRA**. Both of these savings accounts are tax-free as long as the money goes to your child's education. While you can only contribute a maximum of $2,000 per year per child, the payoff can be significant: $2,000 every 18 years yields $36,000. And that doesn't even include the interest! (This time, YOU'RE the one earning a few extra percent!)

Remember, a public four-year school now costs about $14,000 per academic year. One Education IRA easily knocks out two years of that! As if this needed to sound like a better idea, Education IRAs also give your credit and investment reports a boost.

A standard **Roth IRA** can also give you a leg up when it's time to send your kids to school. You can invest up to $4,000 in a Roth IRA every year, which gives it a significantly higher earning potential than you'd get from an Education IRA.

You might also consider looking into the **529 Qualified Tuition Savings Plans.** These plans allow you to invest as much as you'd like. The IRS also considers your contributions to this fund gifts, which will lower your taxes considerably.

529 plans give you a lot more control over your money, but unlike the IRAs, they're not guaranteed. That means that if finance charges change, you may lose principle. A 529 also won't be applicable if your child withdraws form school or earns a scholarship. Sound complicated? It is! In fact, it's so complicated that 529 owners often hire brokers to help with all of the fine print.

No matter how you invest in your child's college education, it is also important to continue saving for yourself. If your child decides not to go to school right away, then you may need to reshuffle some money from the school-oriented savings accounts we've been discussing. In this case, you may want to consider taking out a loan from yourself. In this case, you borrow pre-tax money from one account into another and pay yourself back at a post-tax rate.

Finally, if you haven't invested or haven't invested enough in your child's education, you can take out a **PLUS loan**. Parents of students who are enrolled in school at least half-time are eligible for this form of financial aid. PLUS loans work much like regular student loans, but the repayment is the responsibility of the parent. Sometimes, graduate students take out PLUS loans to pay for Masters' and Doctorate degrees.

The interest rates on PLUS loans can rival those that you'll see on mortgages. They tend to be a large commitment and should be considered as a last resort. Be warned!

Though your financial concerns are probably a little different than those of your child, you ultimately share a goal: getting through college. By doing your research, you can help your child achieve their dreams while also managing your taxes, building credit. Everybody wins!

Chapter 11. The Payoff of Student Loan Consolidation

Why consolidate your student loans? Student loan consolidation allows you to combine all of your federal student loans into a single loan with one monthly payment. Usually, this single payment will be lower than your standard monthly rate.

Consolidating can also allow you to lock in some of the lowest fixed interest rates in recent history. This is a tremendous advantage if you took out student loans whose interest turned out to be greater than you could handle after graduation. In addition to lower monthly rates, consolidating your student loan can also qualify you for new or renewed deferments.

Most consolidated loans have fixed interest rates that are based on the interest rates of the many original loans from which they were formed. Some studies have found that the amount you save up to 58 percent of what you would have paid without consolidating.

Most federal aid, including Federal Stafford loans, Federal Direct Loans, and Federal Perkins loans, qualify for consolidation. Though many federal loans already have low fixed interest rates, this is still a fantastic option to consider.

Before you proceed with consolidation, make certain the rate on your consolidated loan will actually be lower than your current rate. The whole point of consolidation, after all, is to try to make the process of paying student debt easier. Although consolidation does indeed lower your monthly payment, it also can increase the total cost of your student debt. Because consolidated loans may have an amortization of up to 30 years, you might end up making more payments, and therefore pay more in interest. If you don't necessarily need monthly payment relief, you should compare the cost of repaying your unconsolidated loans against the cost of repaying a consolidated loan.

If you do decide to consolidate your student loans, you'll find the process very flexible. Whether you just graduated or have been paying for years, consolidation is always available.

In order to consolidate, you'll need to know the balances and interest rates of all your student loans, the names and addresses of the companies that hold your loans, and the names and addresses of two personal references. If you don't have this information readily available, contact the National Student Loan Data System (NSLDS.) This institution keeps complete and accurate information on federal loans nationwide.

Most student loan consolidation plans present you with two separate repayment options. The first option dictates that you are responsible for paying a certain amount each month. Payments include both principle and balance. This repayment scheme means that you pay back the least total interest.

Graduated repayment is also available as a consolidated loan repayment option. This process begins with low monthly payments that cover the loan's interest only. Later, the monthly payment increases in size, and the principal is included in the amount paid.

Most student consolidation loan repayment begins within 60 days of the loan's disbursement. Amortization is between 10 and 30 years, depending on the amount of student debt being repaid and the repayment plan.

Before you decide to consolidate, be ask your lender a few key questions.

- What plans are available for your income level?

- Are there any opportunities for interest rate reduction?

- Is the lender willing to meet your needs?

- How's the customer service?

- Is this the best possible interest rate?

Be picky! Your lender should be ready and willing to answer all of your questions.

Although most people who want to consolidate their loans have already graduated, you can also consolidate while you're still in school. You must, however, be enrolled at least half time.

Part 5: Credit Cards

Credit cards are a fact of modern life, but they don't need to control your life. Follow this advice to make your cards serve you, and not the other way around.

Chapter 12. Give Yourself a Little Credit: shop for a card with low rates rather than applying for a loan

Want to consolidate your credit card debt? Thinking of buying an expensive home theater? Your first instinct may be to hit up the bank for a loan. But believe it or not, that's not always your best course of action! If you're dealing with debt or making a large purchase, you could consider using your credit card instead.

Despite their obvious dangers, credit cards can be useful financial tools. If you do your research, they can also be a smart alternative to a typical loan.

To put it mildly, credit cards have a bad rap. Though the world of credit cards is definitely tricky, it's only infamous because so many people can't manage their own credit usage. Whether the credit card holder lacks self-control or is just trying to cover out-of-control living expenses, it's easy to rack up thousands of dollars in high-interest credit card debt in a matter of months. Credit cards are not inherently bad; it's the manner in which they are used that makes them dangerous.

No matter what your situation, you CAN avoid the pitfalls of credit cards and make them work for you at the same time.

To begin with, have just a few cards. (Four is ideal.) If you have fewer cards and pay off your entire bill each month, then you'll avoid high interest payments and late fees. If you're already dealing with a lot of credit card debt, switch to a card with a low APR. That way, you'll only have to worry about paying one bill a month.

Choosing a credit card deserves a lot of thought. Of course you're looking for a low interest rate, but is there an additional annual fee? Some credit cards claim that their annual fee lowers your interest, but that may not be the case.

Be extra cautious about "rewards" cards. These incentive deals give you the opportunity to earn "points" toward airfare or a new car. But how is that useful to you if you get one point for every five dollars you spend? After all, there still may be an annual fee – maybe you'll just end up paying back those "rewards" anyway.

Be smart and do your research. Above all, don't be afraid to ask questions! Opening a new credit card can be a serious life decision, and any credit card company that brushes you off is bad news.

Many websites offer free online credit card calculators that allow you to figure out the rate you can afford, how much you can expect to pay, and how annual fees will affect your finances. When you sit down and start figuring out the true cost of credit card debt, you'll probably find yourself looking at some pretty intimidating numbers.

That said, if you run a standard car loan through the same calculator, you might be really shocked at the results. Banks make as much or more on interest than your credit card company does. Bank loans also involve a tedious review process and a great deal of red tape. If you already have a credit card with a high limit and a low interest rate, then why not just use that?

The bank has the advantage of internal discipline, a company structure, and reassuring brick-and-mortar branches where you can count on meeting a human. The set-in-stone payment schedule that bank loans usually feature appeals to many people, too. Credit card companies demand a lot more personal discipline. Usually, the only rule is that you must pay a minimum amount on your credit card debt each month. This figure can be so low that your debt actually continues to grow!

But if this is your only concern, there are ways around it. Thanks to modern technology, you can make automatic payments on your credit card using online banking. This might be a trick you're already familiar with, since many banks allow users to pay everything from rent to water bills automatically. You can even schedule payments for payday so that you're not tempted to overspend. If this is news to you, then talk to your bank about paying your bills over the Internet.

Finally, it's important to shop around. Look at the rates your local bank is offering for loans and see if there is a card that matches it. In the long run, a little legwork could save you a lot of aggravation and money.

Chapter 13: Dealing with Credit Card Debt

Credit cards are a fact of modern life. You usually need one to rent a car or buy online, and plenty of retail outlets incentivize their own credit lines with attractive deals. Having a credit card and regularly paying it off can also make your credit report look good. But credit cards also have a notorious dark side. It's easy to end up with too many credit cards to manage, and a few missed payments can plunge you into debt and ruin your chances of getting a loan.

When you're performing credit report triage, your first step should be to eliminate your extra credit cards. If you have more than four cards open at once, then you're not helping your credit score, and in fact, you run a greater risk of hurting it. This is doubly true if you already have a debt load. Close those extra cards! Four is plenty.

The next most important question is which cards you ought to close. There are a few important factors about closing credit cards that you should know before you take action.

The deceptively important debt-to-credit ratio

First of all, know your debt-to-credit ratio. This number is just your total debt divided by all of the credit you're currently using. Ideally, you want all of your debt to be no greater than half as large as all of your credit. So if you have credit cards that allow you to access a total of $2000 in credit, then you should never have more than $1000 in current credit card debt. That's a ratio of ½, 1 to 2, or 1:2 for short.

This ratio becomes a problem when you want to cancel a credit card. Let's say you want to close a $500 credit line. Once you do that, your total accessible credit will no longer be $2000, but only $1500. Unfortunately, after you close that card, you'll still have that $1000 in debt. Now your debt-to-credit ratio is 1000 divided by 1500 – or 1000/1500 – which boils down to a whopping 2:3! Any lender looking at that ratio is going to think that you're using most of your available credit to sustain your debt, which means that you're a bad risk.

Even though it may be a simply misunderstanding, it's very important to make sure and avoid this trap. Make sure that you get your debt down to where it will need to be *before* you cancel any credit cards. That means that if you know you're only going to have $1500 in credit, make sure that your debt is down to $750 or less *before you cancel that card!* If your debt-to-credit ratio rises higher than 1:2, your lender will not be impressed.

Cancel old cards first

Though your instinct might be to cancel the newer cards – you know, the ones you're not as attached to – it's a much better idea to take out the older ones first. Canceling cards that you've had for less than a year looks bad on your credit report.

Incidentally, it's also good to be develop a consistent pattern of card use over time. If you have several cards, it might be tempting to switch which ones you're using based on payment and interest rates. Resist this urge! Like the rest of your financial history, credit card switching shows up on your credit report, and it looks awful. Instead, develop a good working relationship with your cards. Use them all just enough, not too much, and always pay on time.

Re-establishing yourself after credit card debt

Welcome to the financial problem of the 21st century: re-establishing yourself as a good loan candidate after experiencing credit card debt. While the fallout of your cards may seem enormous, you CAN rebuild your credit.

No matter what's in your past, the easiest way to establish credit is by paying bills on time. This is the single most important factor into your credit score and even making an effort will improve your entire report. This is because your lender's main interest isn't your past, but your future; they want to know that you're financially responsible enough to return their money if and when they loan it to you. Show them you can do it by making every deadline.

If you've never used credit

Enough about reacting to your credit history – what if you've never used credit at all? The answer's pretty simple and involves you not getting a loan. If you don't have any credit history, you're an unknown quantity to lenders. That includes lenders who might give you mortgages, business loans, car loans, and anything else that you'll need to have a comfortable life. Without your credit history, these institutions will have no way of knowing how you manage your finances, and therefore no way to decide whether or not to loan you money. They're likely to play it safe and decline your loan.

You'll need a credit history eventually, no matter what. Now's the time to start building one. The good news is that you know what shows up on your credit report now. You have a priceless once-in-a-lifetime chance to do manage your credit right from the get-go. No low credit score for you! With a little planning, your credit report will shine.

Studying this book will start you out on the right foot. It's worth it to learn everything you can about credit and lending before diving in. Your reward will come to you in the form of better rates, lower interest, and friendly lenders willing to offer you good terms on mortgages and other important loans.

Part 6: Payday Lenders, Loaning to Friends, and Other Special Situations

Life can throw some strange things at average, well-meaning credit holders. These are a few random situations that many people run into while managing their finances.

Chapter 14. Payday Loans REALLY Make You Pay!

Payday lenders are only too eager to help you out. If you're short on money, they will gladly offer you an advance, also known as "fast cash," that will come due when your paycheck arrives. Payday lenders are conveniently located everywhere from the street corner to the Internet. They don't care if your credit is awful, if you have no credit at all, or even if you're completely bankrupt. All they care about is that you have a paying job. To prove that, all you need is proof of employment, a postdated check for the amount you want, and the negligible fee. Then you're in the money. Easy-peasy, right?

There is a saying in business that goes as follows: **THERE IS NO SUCH THING AS A FREE LUNCH.** If someone wants to offer you a loan but doesn't care about your credit score, there's something very wrong.

The APR for payday loans averages 300%. That means that you will definitely pay back *three times* what you borrowed. In fact, you'll probably pay back even more. When you can't make the interest, you'll end up even deeper in debt to the lender. This vicious cycle is tailored to appeal to people who are already in desperate financial circumstances.

As if this wasn't bad enough, this unscrupulous lender also gets your credit report. When you go into debt – as you almost definitely will – that lender will take advantage of any and all of the information on your credit report, including calling up your boss for a friendly chat about your debt. And did we mention that they'll be able to access your checking account?

The long and the short of it is that payday lenders are a nightmare waiting to happen. If you haven't used one yet, DON'T. There are better ways to get money in the short term.

Credit unions, for example, offer small loans under similar conditions as payday lenders. The one critical difference is that the APR on credit union loans are around 15%, so it's more than possible to pay it off. If you already have certain kinds of accounts open at a credit union, you may also be able to borrow from yourself. The upshot is an even lower APR and savings dividends when you pay yourself back.

You might also be able to secure a credit card advance. This isn't an ideal solution because the APR will be between 20% and 25%. Still, that's a long sight better than 300%, and if you're in crisis mode, a credit card advance could save your bacon. Make sure that your credit score can take it, though, and do your best to pay it all back as soon as you have the money.

Finally, never underestimate the resources already available. Ask your banker about overdraft protection. This means that if you write a check without money in your account, the bank automatically gives you a loan. You might also consider talking to your creditors or the source of your most difficult bill. There may be a grace period available, especially if you're only temporarily short on cash.

If you've already fallen into the payday trap, then take heart, because you can get out.

One option is to call the payday lender and tell them that you just don't have the money. Considering that this is the company that gave you $200 and expects $800 back, this might be a long shot. Depending on your situation, though, it could turn up some useful info.

Then, buckle down. No matter what you do, you're in for a rough time. Figure out how much you're going to owe, set up a payment plan, and pay that loan down as fast as possible. This may mean making some major lifestyle adjustments, but we're talking about your freedom here. Isn't it worth it to get a night job or move to a studio apartment? The sooner you're free of that payday loan, the sooner you'll have your life back – and the less that horrific interest rate will hurt you.

After you've eliminated that ugly loan, build yourself a cushion of savings. Make sure you never have to resort to a payday lender again! Sock away six to eight months' income in your savings. It might take a few years to build up, but every time you find yourself getting bored, remember that payday lender.

Almost any alternative is better than borrowing money from a payday lender. Never consider this route!

Chapter 15. Lying About Loans: using loan money for something other than its purpose

When you've accepted a loan for a specific purpose, you are obligated to use it for that purpose. Using that money for anything else is actually illegal, and your lender may even take legal action against you. Even if it hurts, always tell lenders the truth.

Usually when you apply for a loan, the lender will want to know why. Since they need to know that you're not going to waste their money, they'll place restrictions on what you can do with that loan. Student loans will go toward school expenses. Home loans will go toward your home.

Different purposes will come with different rates, fees, and conditions. If you're considered "high risk," for example, there might be less that you can do with your loan. Borrowers who do not have collateral are often considered "high risk," but this varies from lender to lender. Make sure to read the terms and conditions of your contract before you sign.

However, if you plan to use a loan for anything other than its initial purpose, then be aware of the consequences. You'll probably have to give back the loan money or repay it, and a bevy of penalties, right away. You will have incurred a number of fees for breaking the terms of your loan, too. There's also a chance that the lender could sue you, which will cost you even more in lawyers' fees and wasted time. (In contrast, the bank probably won't even notice the expense of a lawsuit.)

Remember, everything you agreed to is written on the application right above your signature. If your dishonesty comes out enough to prompt someone to look into your finances, you're more than likely to be caught red-handed over things like income and assets. At that point, you could face criminal charges for fraud! Now your little lie could balloon into a criminal record, ruined credit, or even jail time. Worth it?

Just don't lie! If you need a loan for general purposes, you are much better off applying for a personal loan. These loans are available through any bank for almost any amount, and you'll have the pleasure and ease of being able to do anything you want with it. You can buy that stereo you've always wanted, purchase a big screen TV, move to a new house, pay your overdue bills, or do pretty much any responsible or irresponsible thing you could possibly want to do with money. There are no restrictions and it's all completely legal.

Of course, you'll still need to pay it back. Sometimes personal loans come with higher interest rates since there is a higher degree of risk involved for the bank. But when it gets right down to it, taking out a personal loan is much better than lying!

Remember there are plenty of loan options available. Even if you keep getting denied, always do the right thing and tell the truth about your intentions. In the end, a few extra dollars in interest will outweigh any court matters.

Chapter 16. Friends Don't Let Friends Loan Money: avoid the pitfalls of loaning to your best friend

Never mix business with pleasure. There are many excellent reasons that many people prefer to keep their social lives and their finances separate. Poor business decisions, bad ventures, or unpaid loans can destroy a friendship.

When there is no one else to turn to, accepting help from a friend can be tempting. The same goes for offering help to a buddy in a bind. What are friends for?

Even if you feel like a jerk, it's healthiest to either look at a friend-to-friend loan as a business transaction or just not make one.

Eliminate All Other Options

Are there no other options available? If one bank won't help, try the others. Whoever is taking the loan should be able to produce a monthly budget, bare their finances, and have a repayment plan up front. Whether it's you or your friend who needs cash, all nonessentials must be removed before this loan is even a serious idea. If more money turns up than expected, or elimination of a few luxuries will cover the needs at hand, then this loan is not happening.

Treat it Like the Business Arrangement it is

Most people fail to treat a friend-to-friend loan like the business arrangement it is. Outline in writing the amount being borrowed, the time frame for repayment and the amount of interest (if any) that will be included in the repayment. If you do not have a solid agreement in writing, confusion and heartache will ensue.

Spend wisely when you borrow from a friend

This may seem obvious, but you'd be surprised how much of a problem this can become. Most people don't mind helping out a friend, but it can be very aggravating to discover that the loaned money is being misspent. After all, the first priority should be repaying the loan. That's the friendly thing to do!

Communication is key. Both of you know that the money must be paid back, but not talking about it can cause frustration and confusion. Both people should must voice their feelings about the loan before things get awkward.

Pay it back!

No matter how long it takes, this loan must be repaid. Now it's not just money on the line, but a friend. If repayment takes longer than anticipated, then communicate, communicate, communicate. Make absolutely sure that everybody understands the circumstances. Most people will understand if there are good reasons for the delay.

Even if the friendship ends before the loan is repaid, it's still important to return all the money. Even though friend loans don't show up on credit reports, your good name will suffer if you hold out.

Conclusion

Congratulations! You've made it through this brief review of credit and loans. There's much more to know, but now you can consider yourself ready to deal with the basics of loan and credit application.

Remember, a proper lender will be more than happy to talk about everything you read here and more. Ask questions! Never sign for a loan unless you completely understand everything about it.

Good luck!

We Want Your Feedback on This Book!

Our main purpose is to make sure that our readers get value from the books we publish and that they have a good experience with all of our products. We are always working to improve our books and other products with every revision and update.

Every piece of feedback makes a difference in this process. And we would appreciate yours as well - whether it is good or bad.

Please take one minute to let us know what you thought by following this link:

http://checkmatemg.com/feedbackloans/

www.ingramcontent.com/pod-product-compliance
Lightning Source LLC
Chambersburg PA
CBHW071824170526
45167CB00003B/1411